DINOSAURS WITH JOBS
a coloring book celebrating our old-school coworkers

drawn and written by
Theo Nicole Lorenz

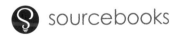 sourcebooks

Originally published as *Dinosaurs with Jobs* in 2013 in the United States by Theo Nicole Lorenz with the CreateSpace Independent Publishing Platform.

Published by Sourcebooks, Inc.
P.O. Box 4410, Naperville, Illinois 60567-4410
(630) 961-3900
Fax: (630) 961-2168
www.sourcebooks.com

Printed and bound in the United States of America.
VP 10 9 8 7 6 5 4 3 2 1

Disclaimer 1: A few of the creatures shown in this book are not, technically speaking, dinosaurs. Plesiosaurus and ichthyosaurus are prehistoric marine reptiles, and pterodactyl is a prehistoric flying reptile. The artist apologizes for any confusion caused by their inclusion.

Disclaimer 2: The artist is not actually sorry for including them, though, because they're awesome and were super fun to draw.

Disclaimer 3: You probably shouldn't be relying on coloring books about dinosaur employment for your scientific education, anyway. Go to the library.

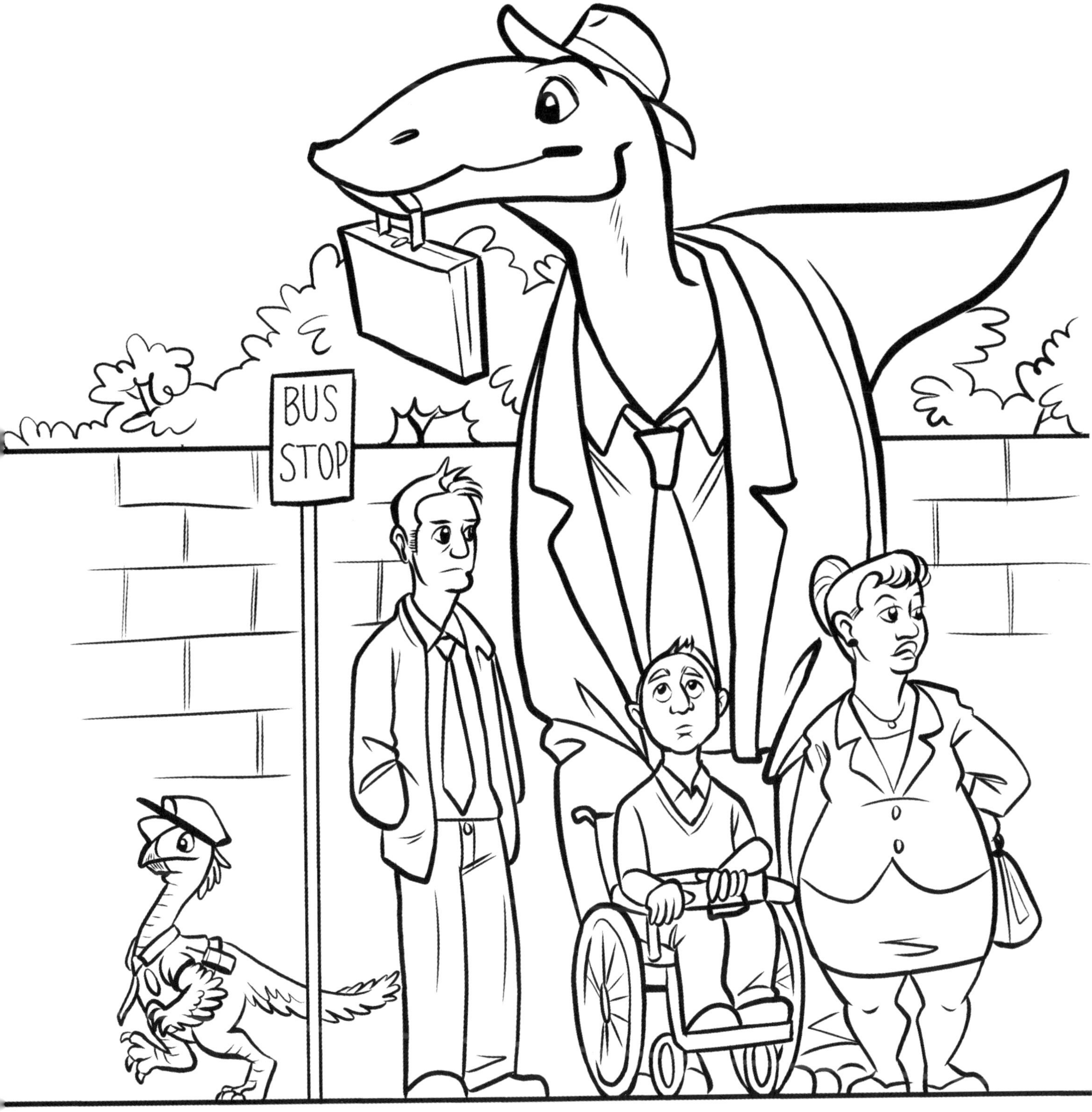
BUS
STOP

Dinosaurs are an important part of our workforce.

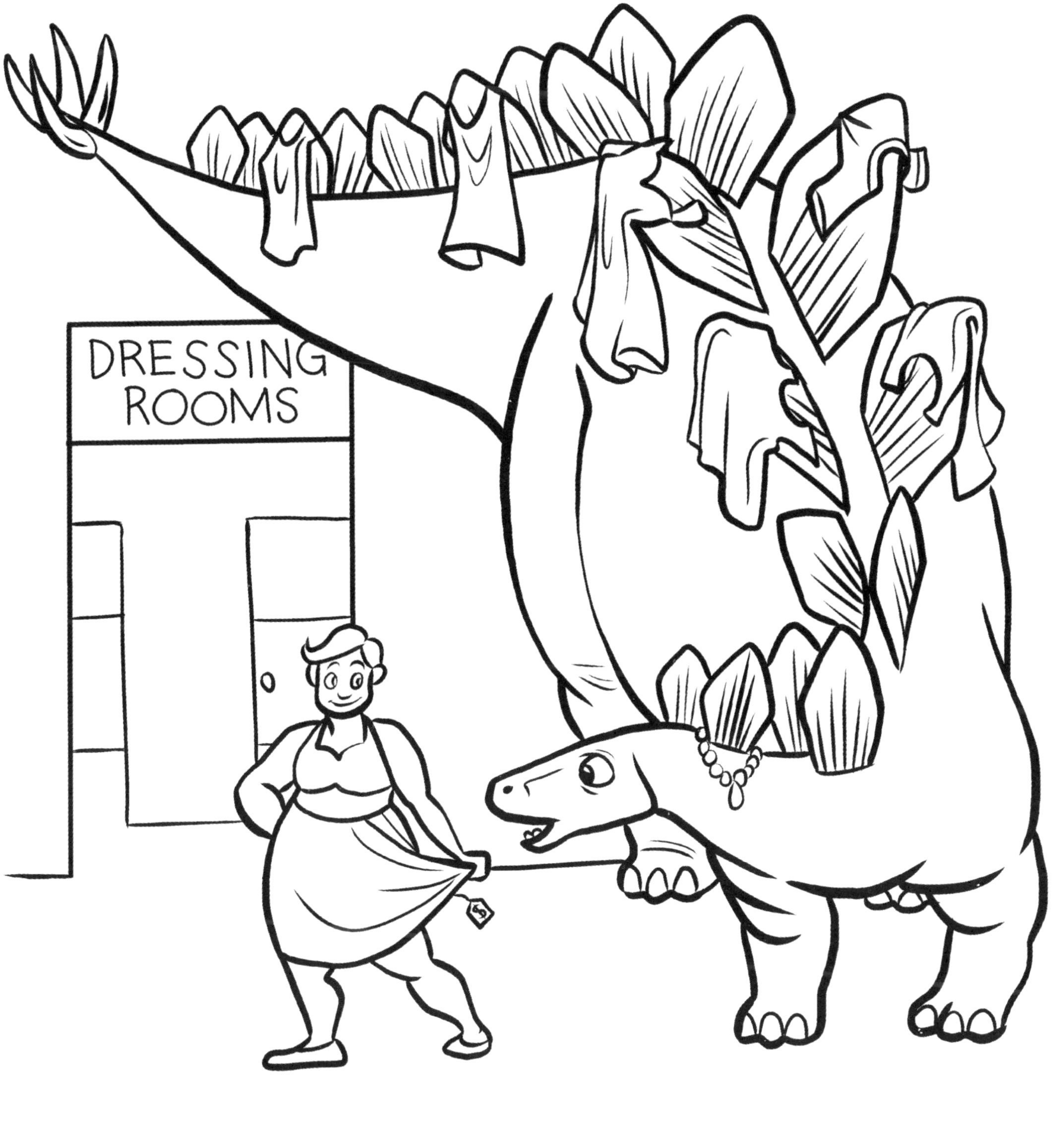
DRESSING
ROOMS

Stegosaurus works in a clothing store and enjoys being helpful.

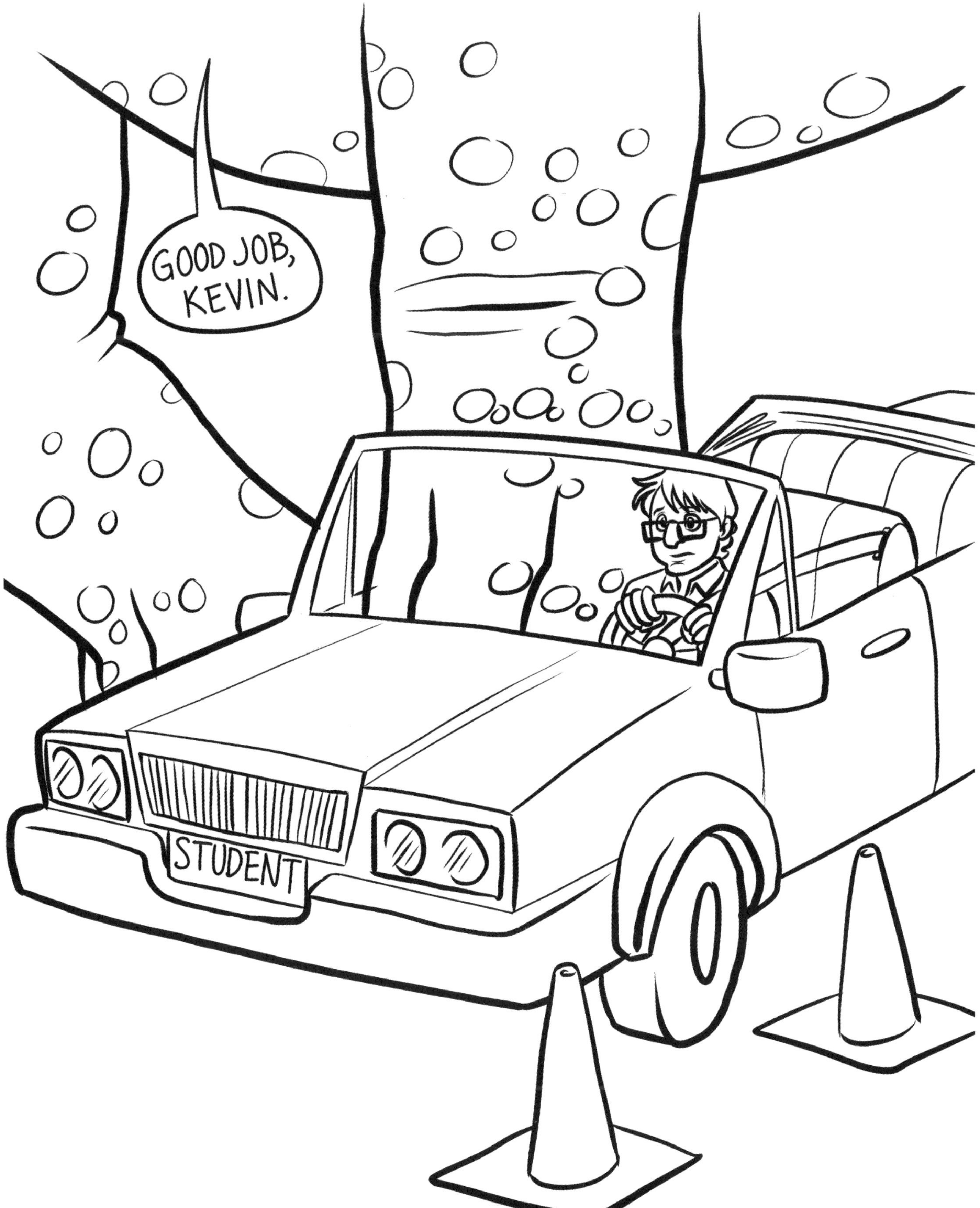
GOOD JOB, KEVIN.
STUDENT

Argentinosaurus is one of the world's largest dinosaurs and the world's largest driving instructor.

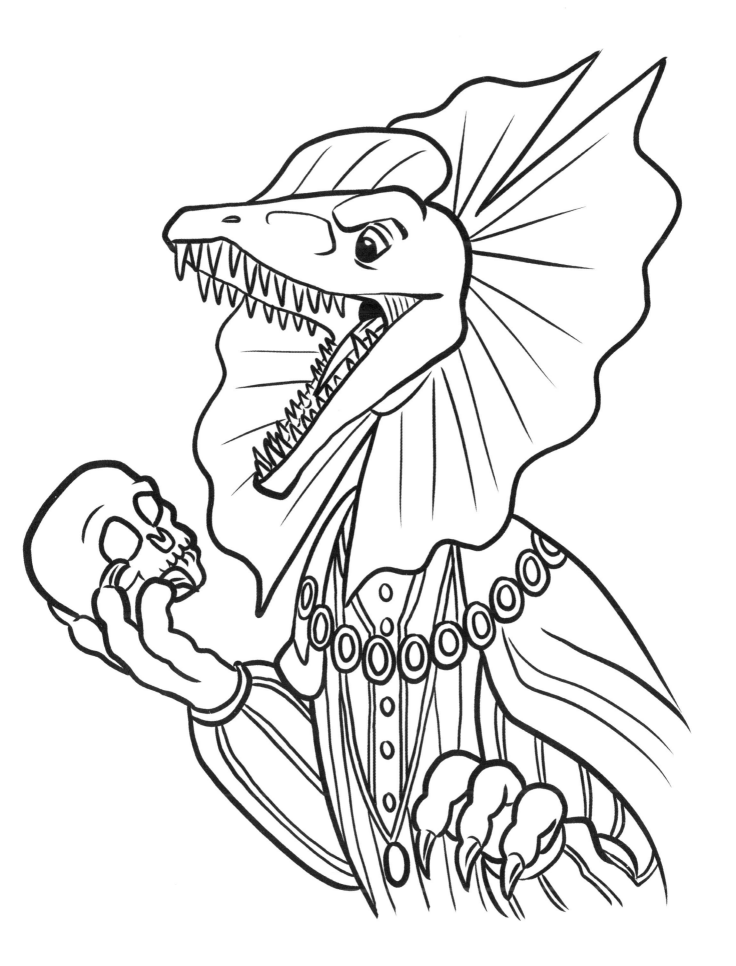

Dilophosaurus is a classically trained Shakespearean actor.

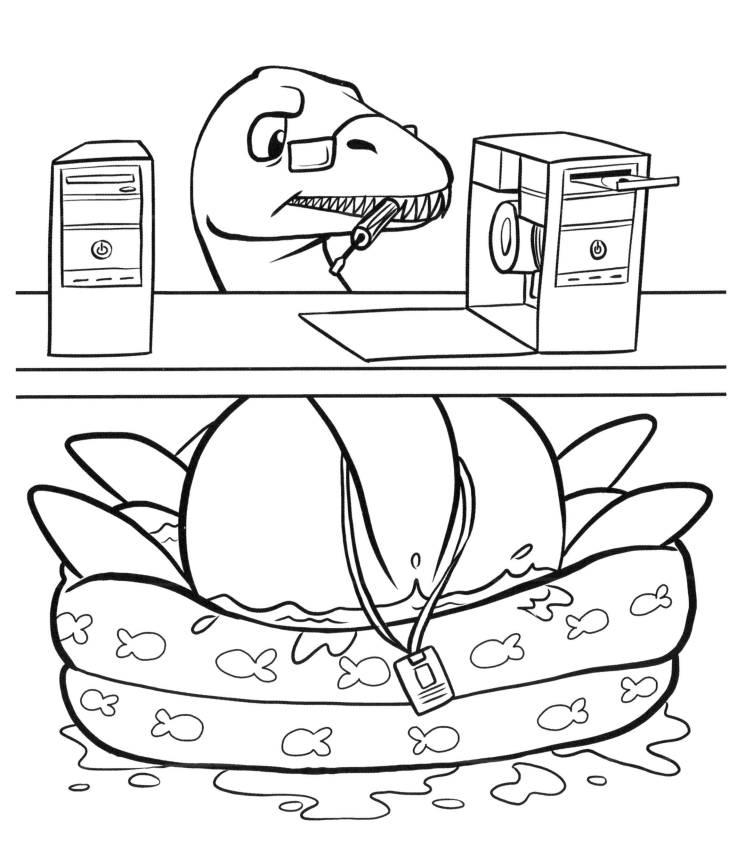

Plesiosaurus tech support specialist would like to remind you that the CD drive is NOT a cup holder.

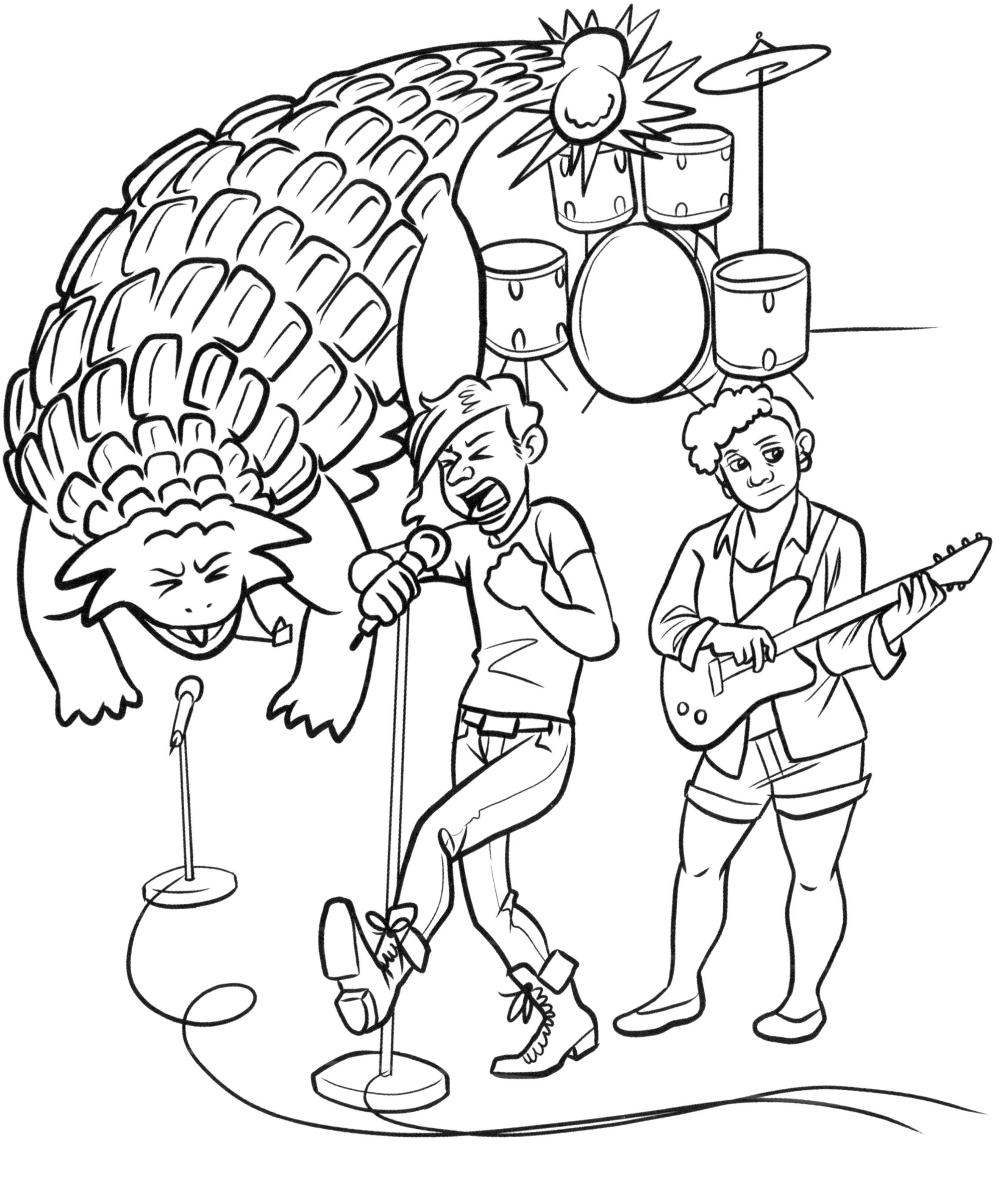

Ankylosaurus's band is going to make it big any day now.

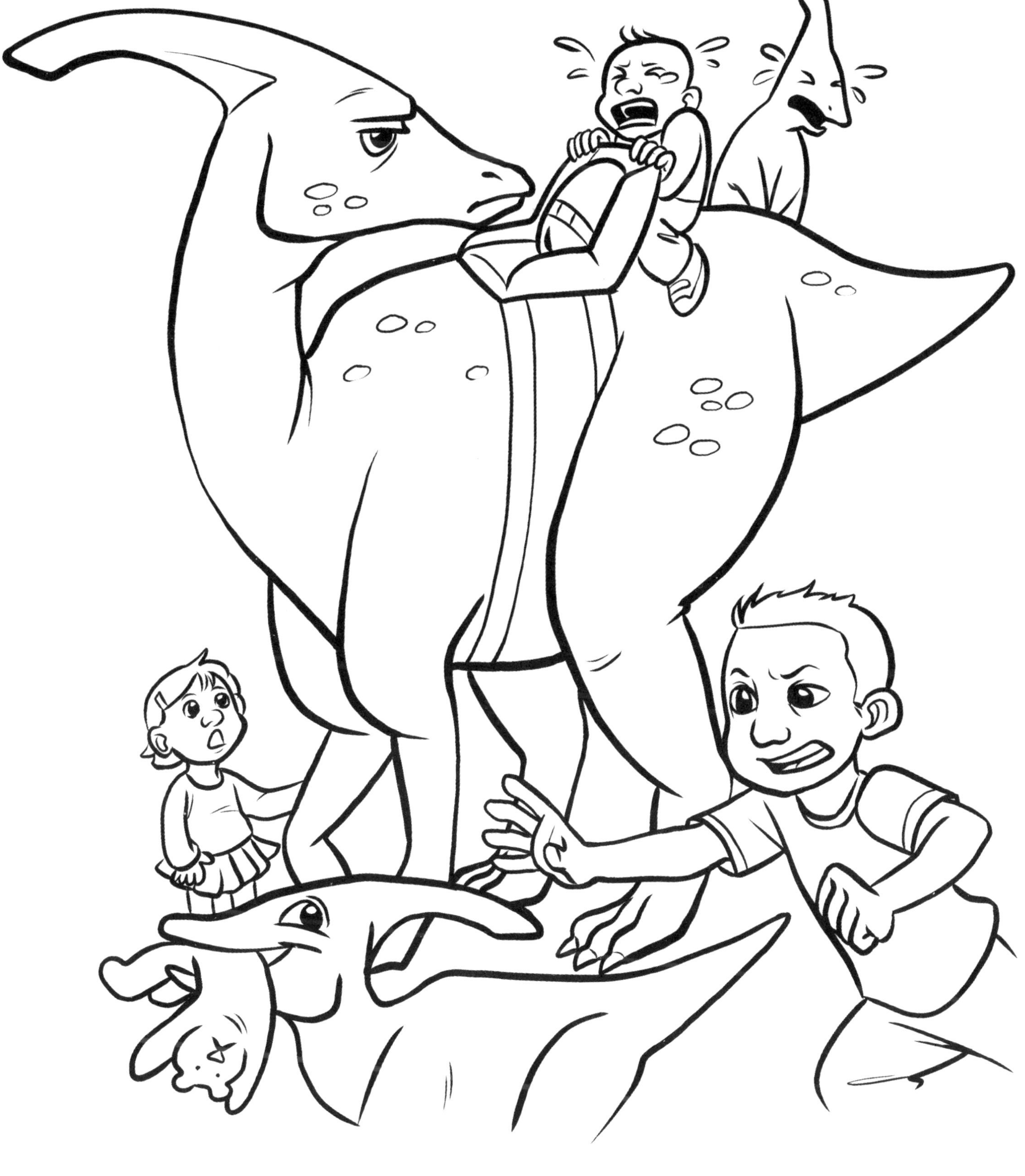

Being a stay-at-home parent is rewarding,
but Parasaurolophus wishes it came with paid time off.

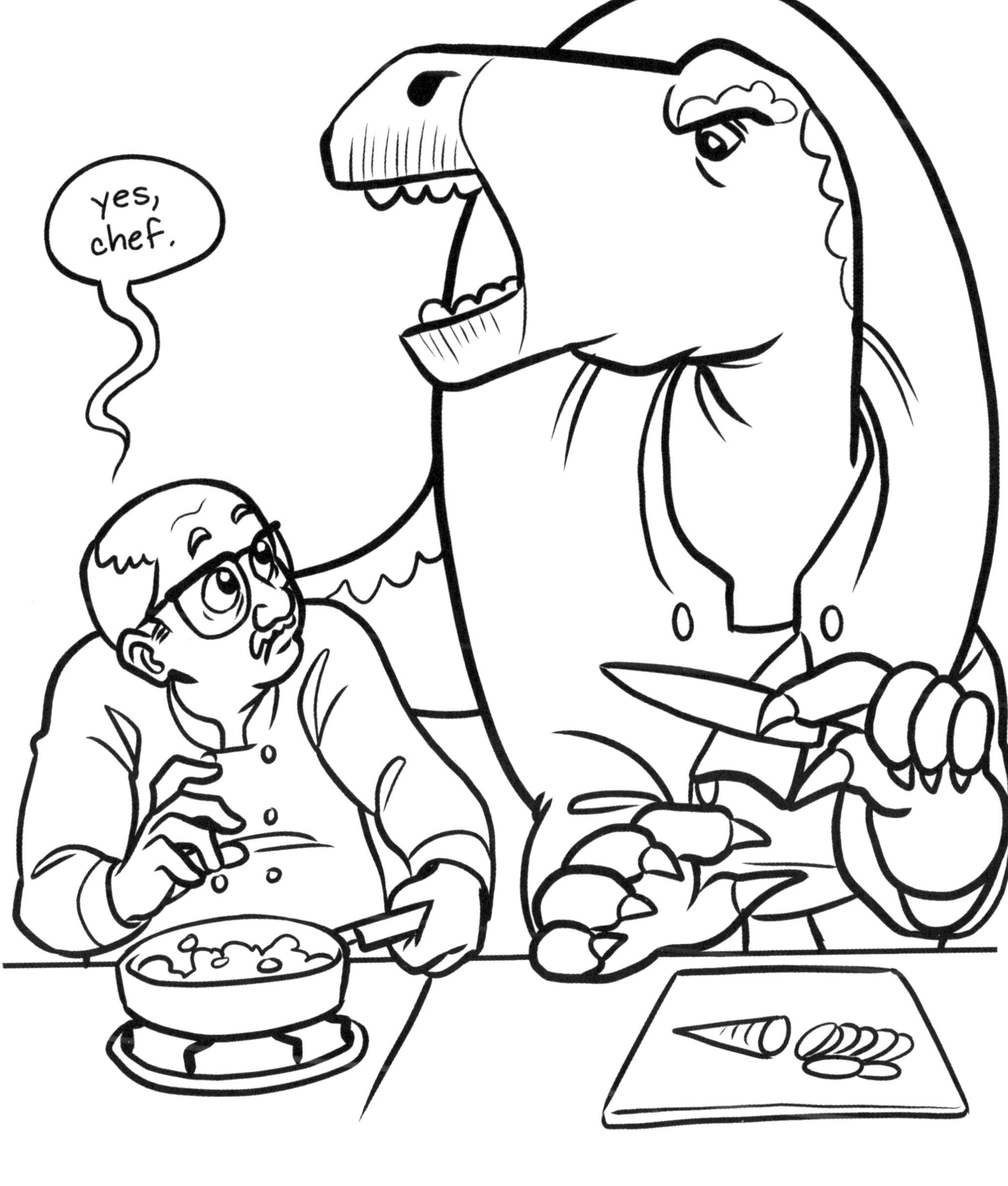
yes, chef.

Iguanodon is a celebrity chef with his own reality TV show.

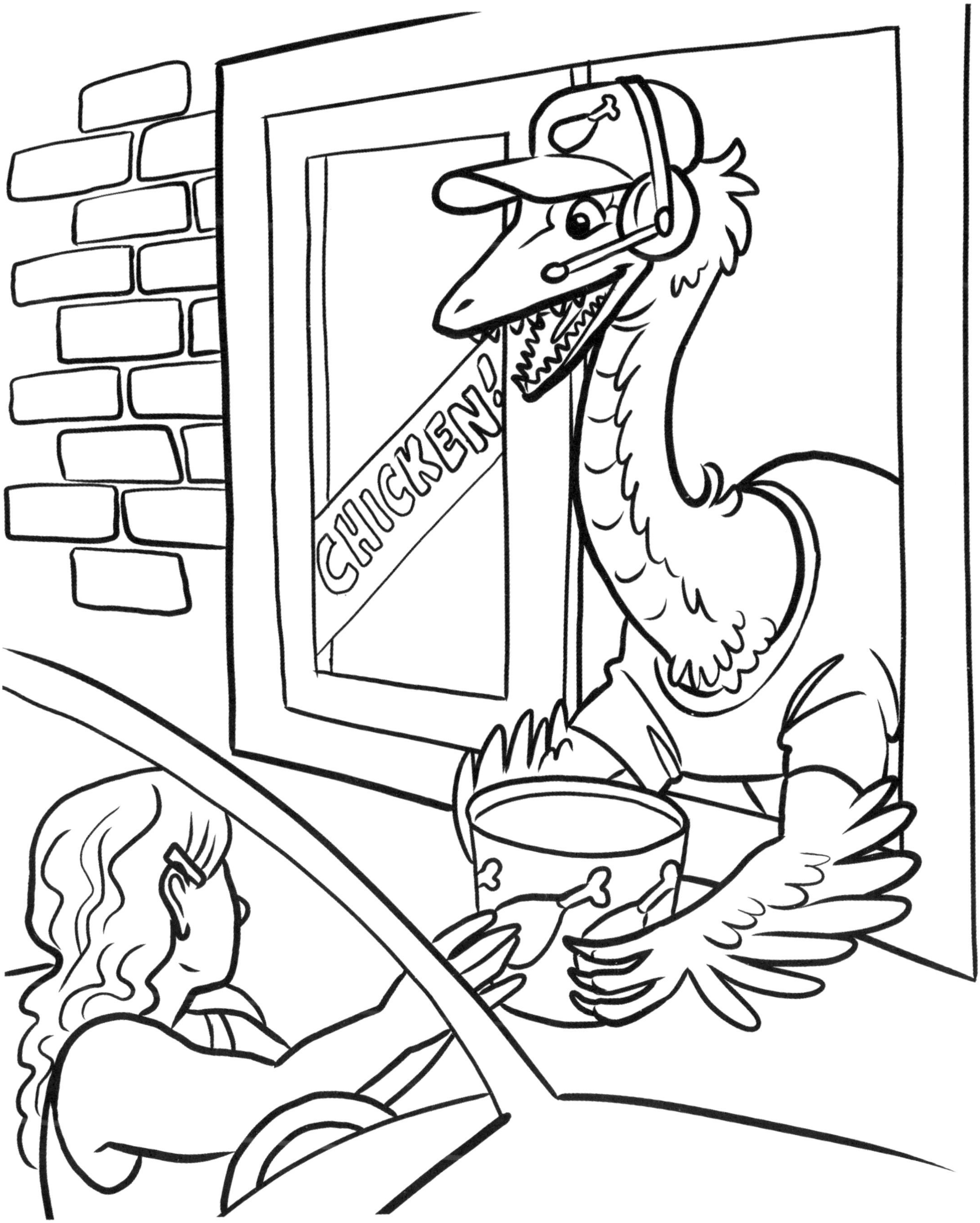
CHICKEN!

Ornithomimus works the drive-through window
and gets all the fried chicken she can eat.

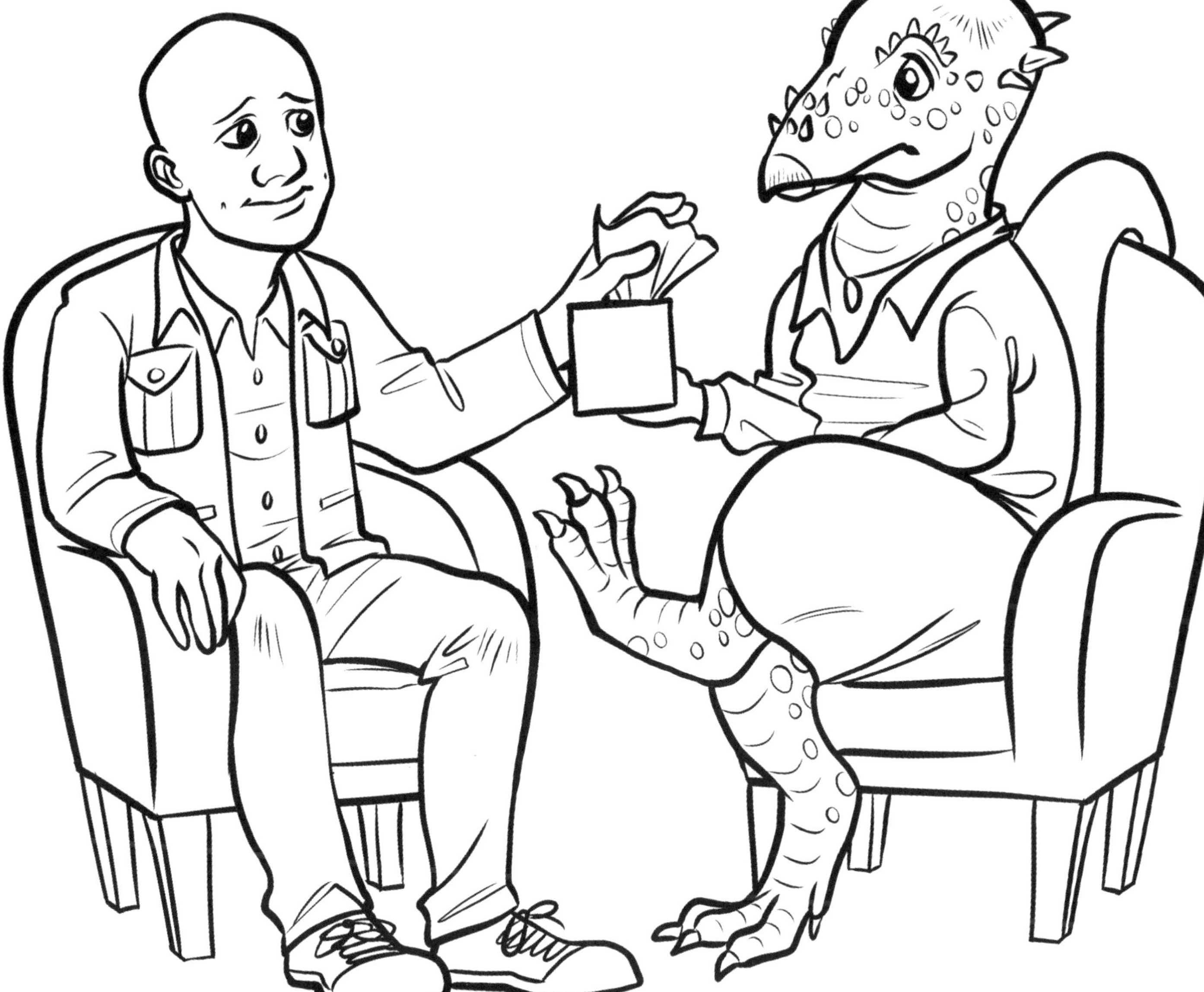

Pachycephalosaurus uses empathy instead of head-butting to help clients at her therapy practice.

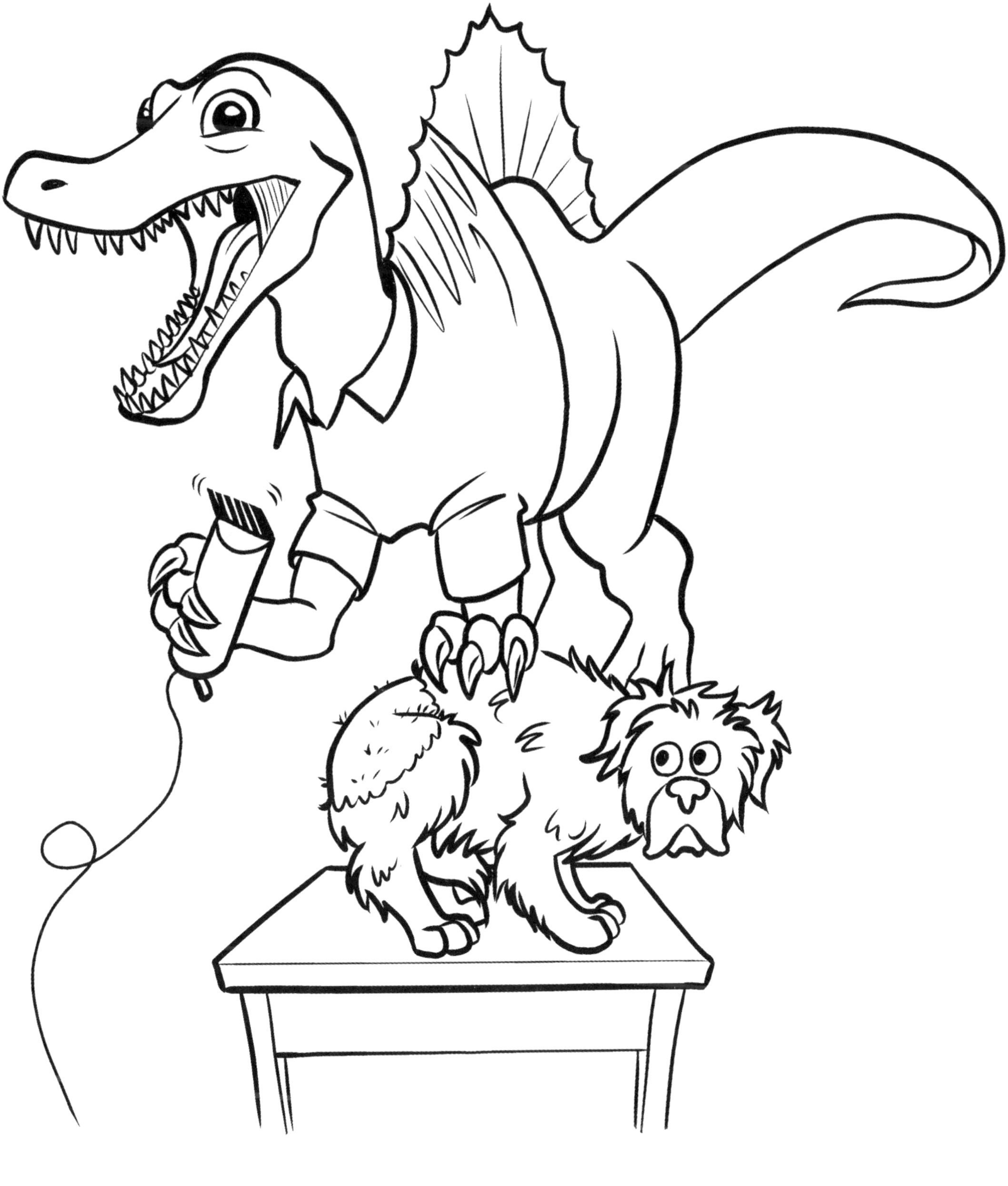

Spinosaurus loves working with animals
at the pet grooming shop!

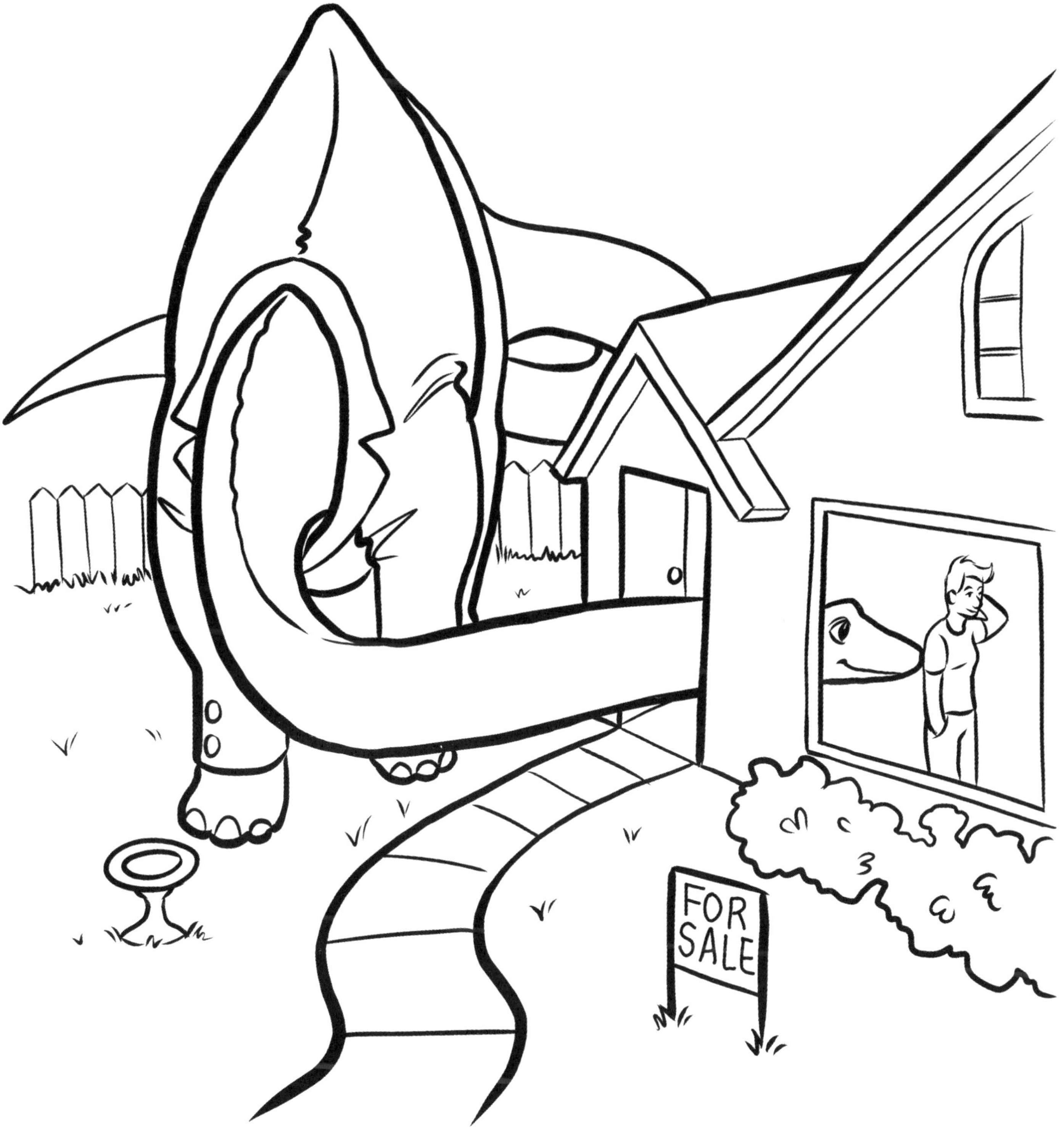
FOR SALE

Despite the fact that she can't actually fit inside a house, Apatosaurus is one of the top real estate agents in the area.

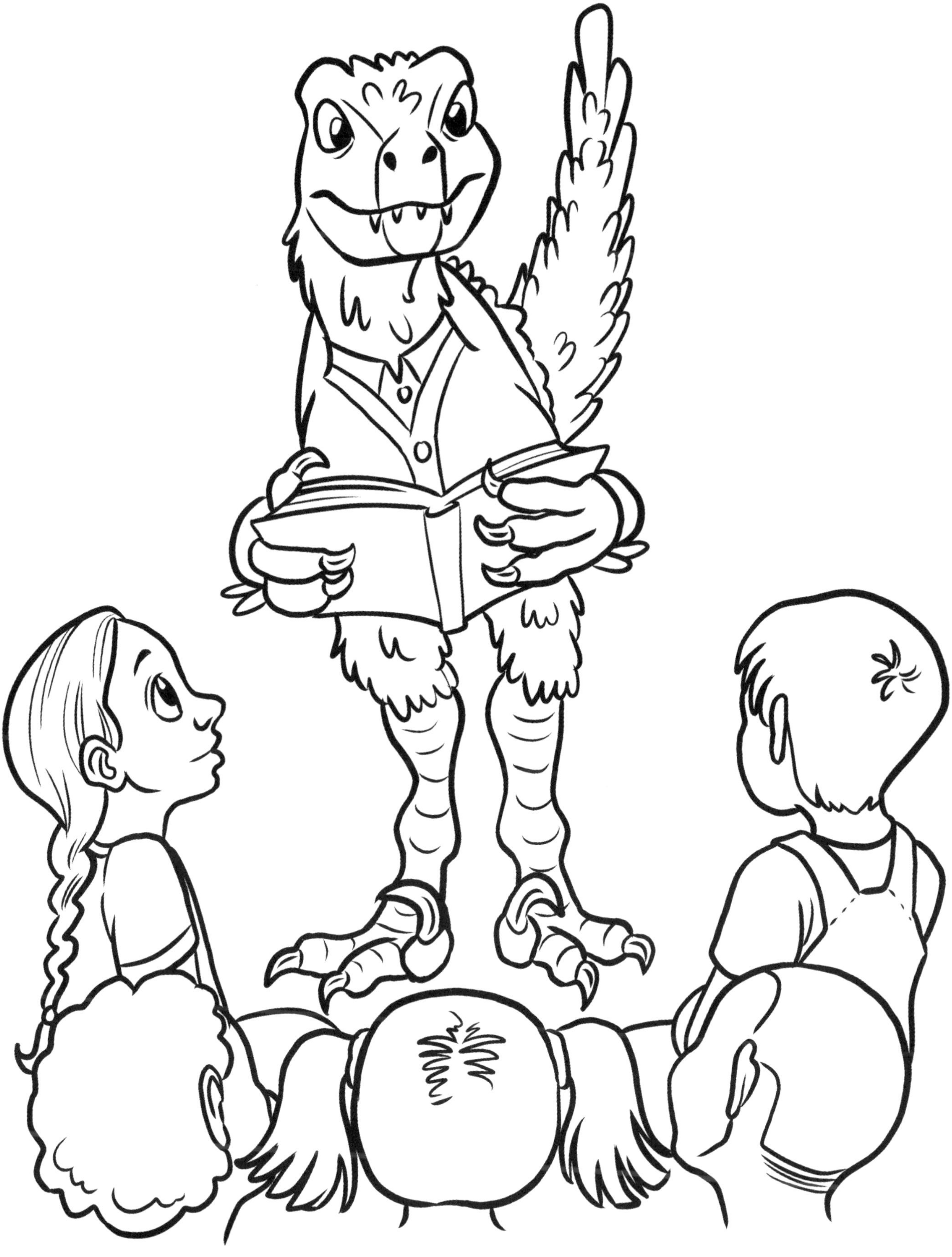

Velociraptor teaches the most well-behaved
kindergarten class this school has ever seen.

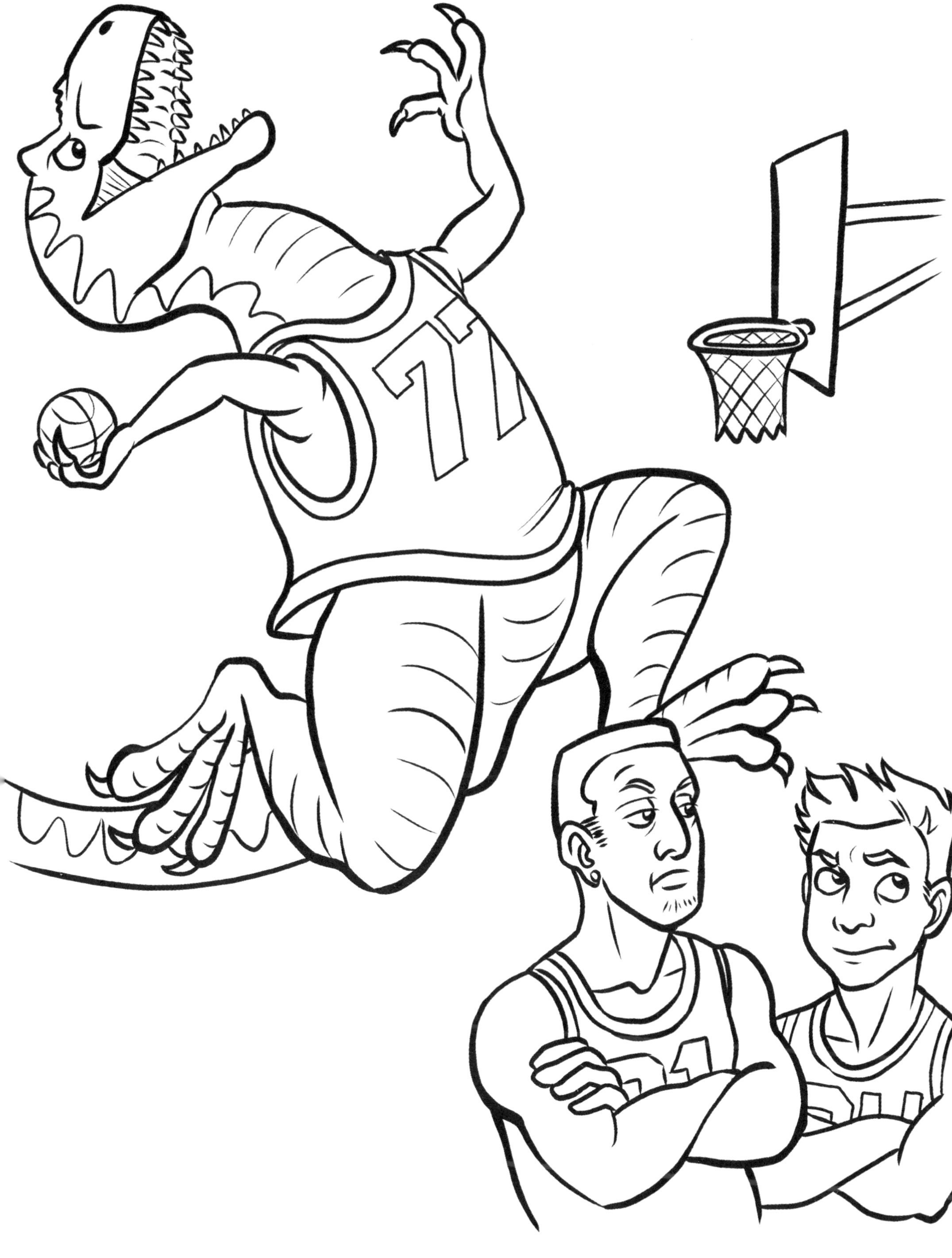
77

Allosaurus has been even more of a show-off since he landed his big pro basketball contract.

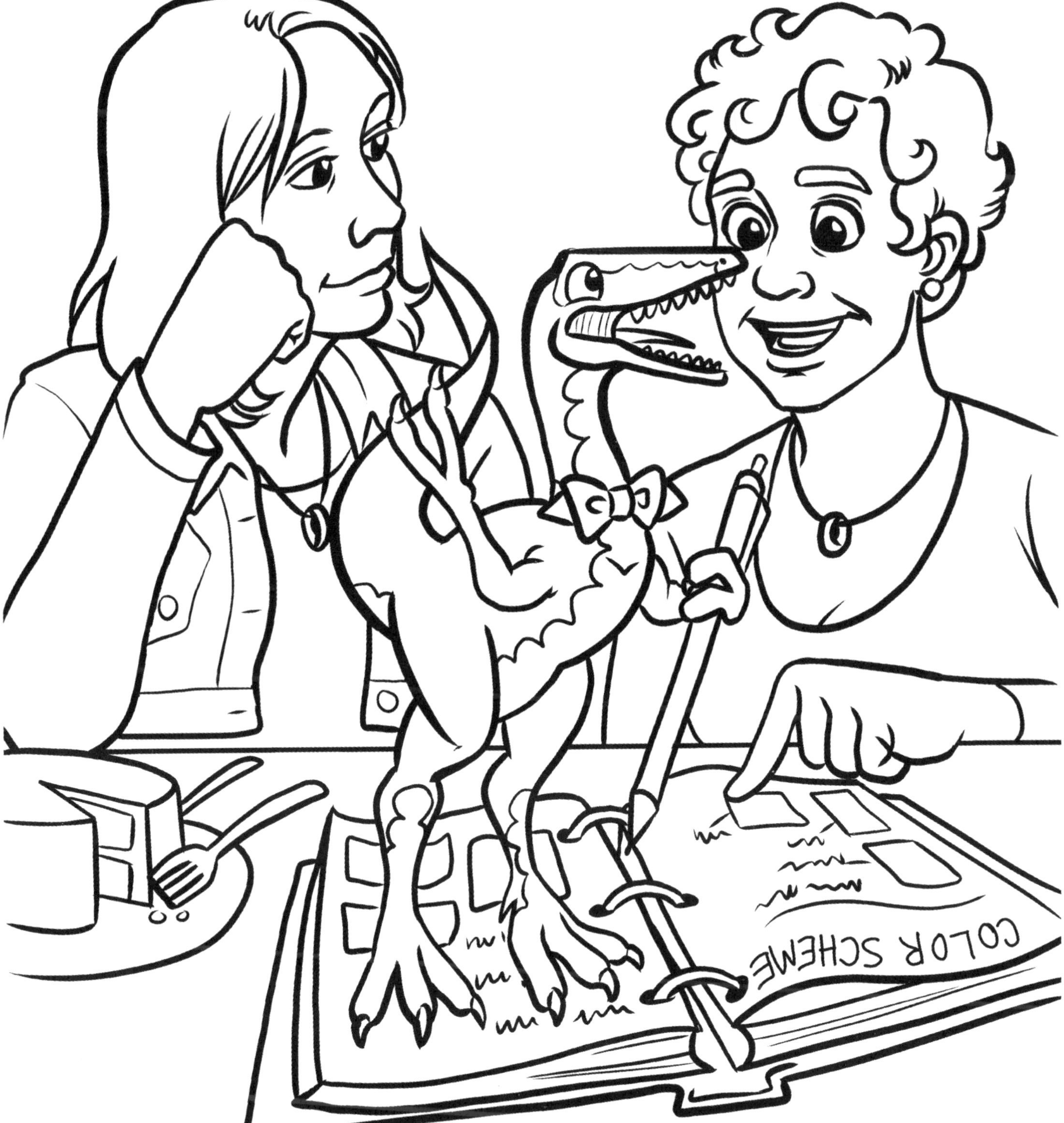
COLOR SCHEME

Compsognathus channeled his enthusiasm and flair
into a career as a wedding planner.

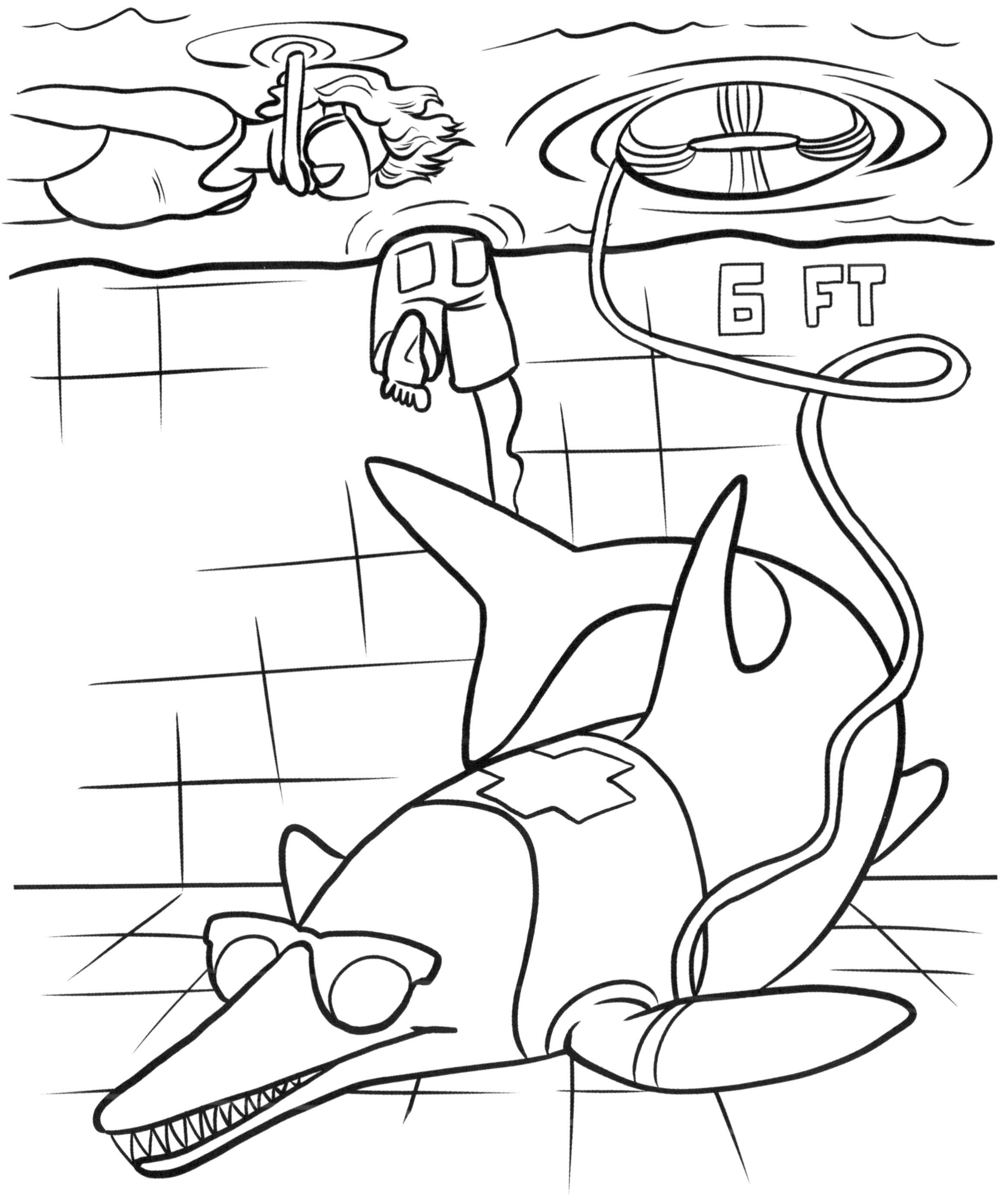
6 FT

Ichthyosaurus found her dream job:
working as a lifeguard at the local pool.

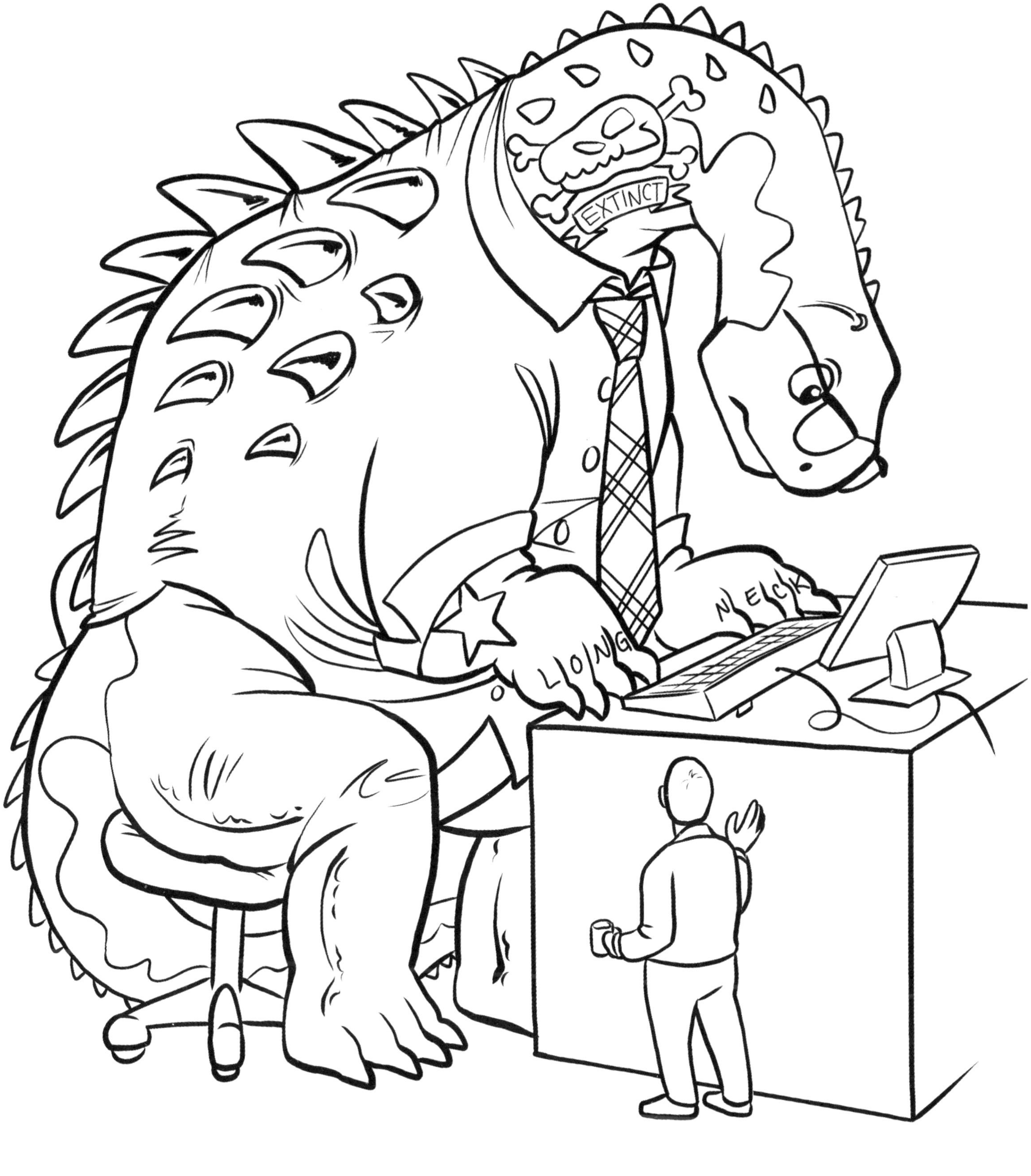
EXTINCT
LONG
NECK

Ampelosaurus balances a career in accounting
with a punk rock lifestyle.

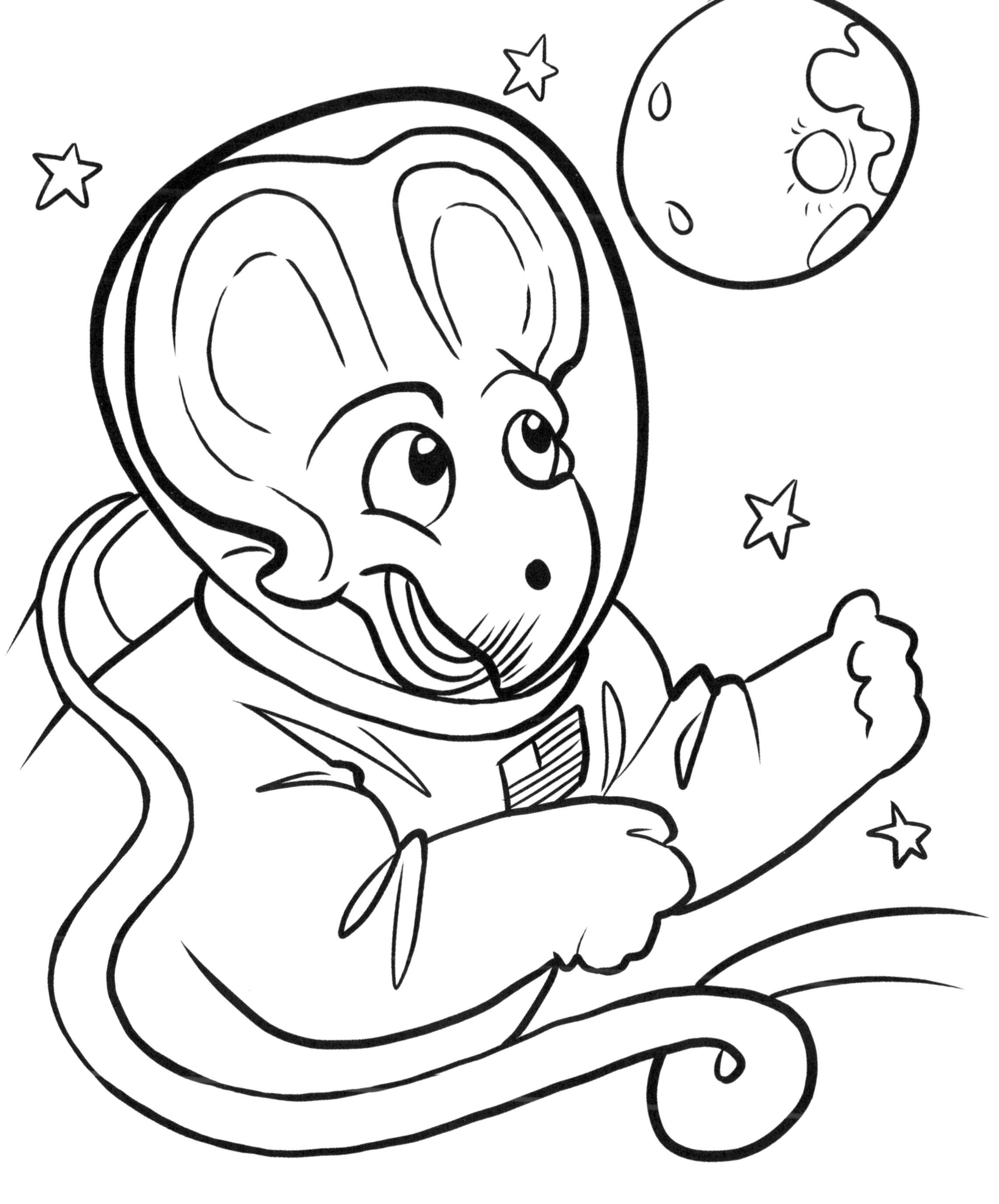

Protoceratops is the first Cretaceous creature in space!

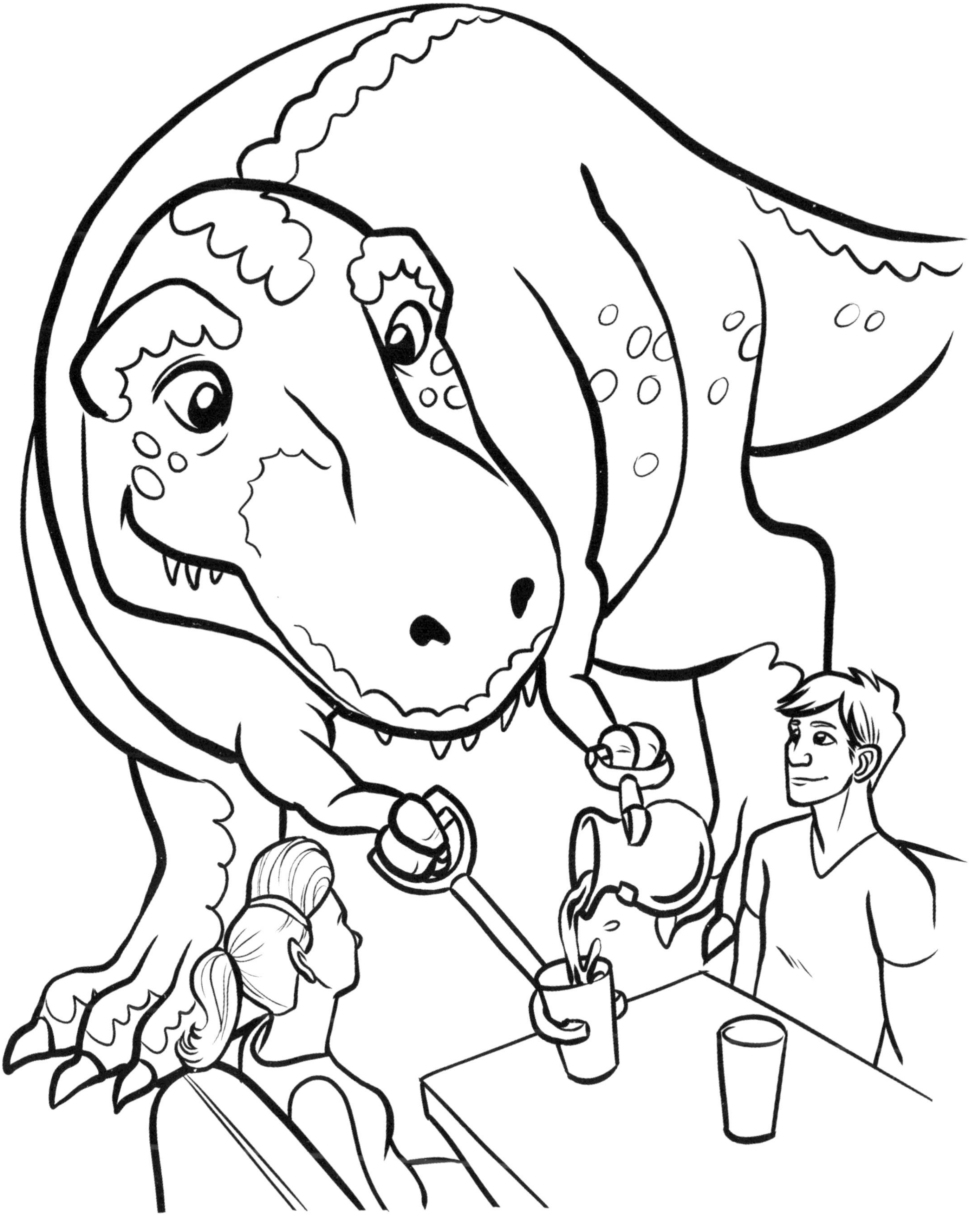

Everyone told Tyrannosaurus he could never be a waiter because of his little arms, but he makes it work.

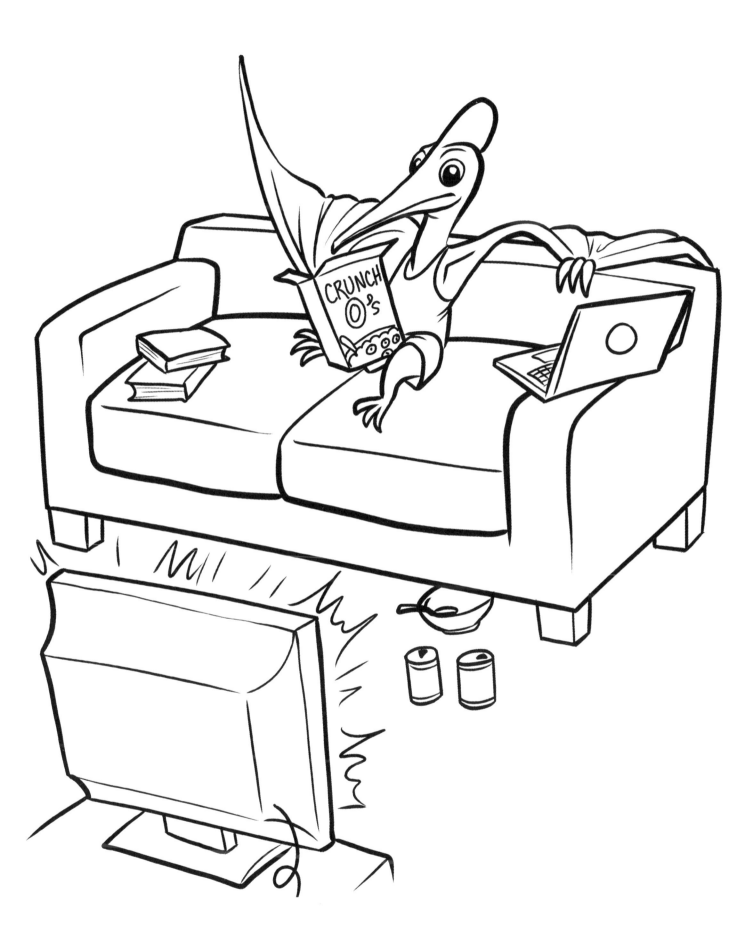

Pterodactyl is unemployed at the moment,
so she's applying for jobs and watching crime dramas.

About the Artist

Theo is an artist, writer, and coloring book tycoon who lives in Saint Paul, Minnesota, with her stegosaurus assistant, Steve. She has an MFA in creative writing from Hamline University.

Dinosaurs With Jobs is her third coloring book, following *Fat Ladies in Spaaaaace: a body-positive coloring book* and *Unicorns Are Jerks: a coloring book exposing the cold, hard, sparkly truth*. For more of Theo's work visit www.theonicole.com.

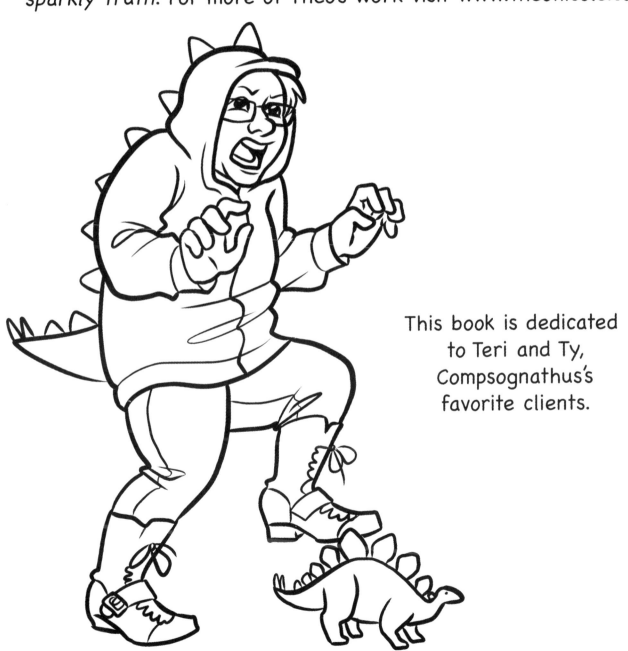

This book is dedicated to Teri and Ty, Compsognathus's favorite clients.